Step-by-Step, Practical Recipes Cooking on a Budget: Contents

Fish Dishes

Packed with flavour, these recipes offer a tasty yet economical way to enjoy this nutritious food group.

Meat & Poultry

Who said meat was too pricey to cook on a budget? Let these hearty dishes do the talking!

Vegetables & Vegetarian

Colourful, versatile and incredibly healthy, these vegetable-based meals delight the tastebuds as well as the bank balance.

Baking & Desserts

Budgeting doesn't have to mean boring – home-baked treats save money and they taste delicious.

FLAME TREE has been creating family-friendly, classic and beginner recipes for our bestselling cookbooks for over 20 years now. Our mission is to offer you a wide range of expert-tested dishes, while providing clear images of the final dish so that you can match it to your own results. We hope you enjoy this super selection of recipes – there are plenty more to try! Titles in this series include:

Cupcakes • Slow Cooker • Curries Soups & Starters • Baking & Breads Cooking on a Budget • Winter Warmers Party Cakes • Meat Eats • Party Food Chocolate • Sweet Treats

www.flametreepublishing.com

Smoked Haddock Tart

INGREDIENTS

Serves 6

For the shortcrust pastry:

150 g/5 oz plain flour

pinch salt

25 g/1 oz white vegetable fat,
  cut into small cubes

40 g/1½ oz butter or hard margarine,
  cut into small cubes

For the filling:

225 g/8 oz smoked haddock,
  skinned and cubed

2 large eggs, beaten

300 ml/½ pint single cream

1 tsp Dijon mustard

freshly ground black pepper

125 g/4 oz Gruyère cheese, grated

1 tbsp freshly snipped chives

To serve:

lemon wedges

tomato wedges

fresh green salad leaves

1. Preheat the oven to 190°C/375°F/Gas Mark 5, 10 minutes before baking. To make the pastry, sift the flour and salt into a large bowl. Add the fats and mix lightly. Using the fingertips, rub into the flour until the mixture resembles breadcrumbs. Sprinkle 1 tablespoon cold water into the mixture and, with a knife, start bringing the dough together. (It may be necessary to use the hands for the final stage.) If the dough does not form a ball instantly, add a little more water. Put the pastry in a polythene bag and chill for at least 30 minutes.

2. On a lightly floured surface, roll out the pastry and use to line an 18 cm/7 inch, lightly oiled quiche or flan tin. Prick the base all over with a fork and bake blind in the preheated oven for 15 minutes.

3. Carefully remove the pastry from the oven and brush with a little of the beaten egg. Return to the oven for a further 5 minutes, then place the fish in the pastry case.

4. For the filling, beat together the eggs and cream. Add the mustard, black pepper and cheese and pour over the fish. Sprinkle with the chives and bake for 35–40 minutes until the filling is golden brown and set in the centre. Serve hot or cold with the lemon and tomato wedges and salad leaves.

1

3

4

Luxury Fish Pasties

INGREDIENTS

Serves 4

75 g/3 oz margarine or butter
75 g/3 oz plain flour
250 ml/8 fl oz milk
175 g/6 oz salmon fillet, skinned
  and cut into small pieces
1 tbsp freshly chopped parsley
1 tbsp freshly chopped dill
grated zest and juice of 1 lime
75 g/3 oz peeled prawns,
  thawed if frozen
salt and freshly ground black pepper
350 g/12 oz ready-made puff pastry
1 small egg, beaten
1 tsp sea salt
fresh green salad leaves, to serve

1. Preheat the oven to 200°C/400°F/Gas Mark 6. Place the margarine or butter in a saucepan and heat slowly until melted. Add the flour and cook, stirring, for 1 minute. Remove from the heat and gradually add the milk a little at a time, stirring after each addition.

2. Return to the heat and simmer, stirring continuously, until thickened. Remove from the heat and add the salmon, parsley, dill, lime zest, lime juice, prawns and seasoning.

3. Roll out the pastry on a lightly floured surface and cut out four 12.5 cm/5 inch circles and 4 x 15 cm/6 inch circles. Brush the edges of the smaller circles with the beaten egg and place two tablespoons of the filling in the centre of each one.

4. Place the larger circles over the filling and press the edges together to seal. Pinch the edge of the pastry between the forefinger and thumb to ensure a firm seal and decorative edge.

5. Cut a slit in each parcel, brush with the beaten egg and sprinkle with sea salt. Transfer to a baking sheet and cook in the preheated oven for 20 minutes, or until golden brown. Serve immediately with some fresh green salad leaves.

HELPFUL HINT

If you require fresh fish for your dish, it is a good idea to visit a busy fishmonger – they will have a high turnover and therefore a fresh supply.

2

3

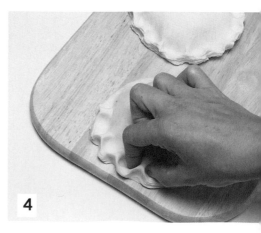

4

Smoked Haddock Kedgeree

INGREDIENTS

Serves 4

300 g/10 oz smoked haddock fillets
50 g/2 oz margarine or butter
1 onion, peeled and finely chopped
2 tsp mild curry powder
175 g/6 oz long-grain rice
450 ml/³⁄₄ pint fish or vegetable
  stock, heated
2 large eggs, hard-boiled and shelled
2 tbsp freshly chopped parsley
salt and freshly ground black pepper
pinch cayenne pepper

1 Place the haddock in a shallow frying pan and cover with 300 ml/¹⁄₂ pint water. Simmer gently for 8–10 minutes until the fish is cooked.

2 Drain, then remove all the skin and bones from the fish and flake into a dish. Keep warm.

3 Melt the margarine or butter in a saucepan and add the chopped onion and curry powder. Cook, stirring, for 3–4 minutes until the onion is soft, then stir in the rice. Cook for a further minute, stirring continuously, then stir in the hot stock.

4 Cover and simmer gently for 15 minutes, or until the rice has absorbed all the liquid. Cut the eggs into quarters and add half to the mixture with half the parsley.

5 Carefully fold the cooked fish into the mixture. Season to taste with salt and pepper. Heat the kedgeree through until piping hot.

6 Transfer the mixture to a large dish and garnish with the remaining quartered eggs and parsley and serve sprinkled with cayenne pepper. Serve immediately.

HELPFUL HINT

If you find undyed smoked haddock rather than the brightly coloured yellow type, you may well find the texture and flavour are better.

2

3

4

Spanish Omelette with Smoked Cod

INGREDIENTS

Serves 3–4

125 g/4 oz smoked cod

3 tbsp sunflower oil

350 g/12 oz potatoes, peeled and cut
   into 1 cm/½ inch cubes

2 onions, peeled and cut into wedges

2–4 large garlic cloves, peeled
   and thinly sliced

1 large red pepper, deseeded,
   quartered and thinly sliced

25 g/1 oz margarine or butter, melted

6 eggs, beaten

salt and freshly ground black pepper

2 tbsp freshly chopped
   flat-leaf parsley

50 g/2 oz mature Cheddar
   cheese, grated

To serve:

crusty bread

tossed green salad

1 Place the cod in a shallow dish and pour over boiling water. Leave for 5 minutes, then drain and allow to cool. When cool, discard the skin and any pin bones and cut into small pieces.

2 Heat the oil in a large, nonstick, heavy-based frying pan, add the potatoes, onions and garlic and cook gently for 10–15 minutes until golden brown, then add the red pepper. Place the cod on top of the vegetables and cook for 3 minutes.

3 When the vegetables are cooked, drain off any excess oil. Beat the margarine or butter into the eggs, season, then stir in the parsley. Pour the egg mixture over the top of the vegetables and cod and cook gently for 5 minutes, or until the eggs become firm.

4 Sprinkle the grated cheese over the top and place the pan under a preheated hot grill. Cook for 2–3 minutes until the cheese is golden and bubbling. Carefully slide the omelette onto a large plate and serve immediately with plenty of bread and salad.

Pork Fried Noodles

INGREDIENTS

Serves 4

125 g/4 oz dried thread egg noodles
125 g/4 oz broccoli florets
2 tbsp groundnut oil
300 g/10 oz pork tenderloin,
   cut into slices
3 tbsp soy sauce
1 tbsp lemon juice
pinch sugar
1 tsp chilli sauce
2.5 cm/1 inch piece fresh root ginger,
   peeled and cut into sticks
1 garlic clove, peeled
   and chopped
1 green chilli, deseeded
   and sliced
25 g/1 oz mangetout, halved
2 medium eggs, lightly beaten

To garnish:
radish rose
spring onion curls

1 Place the noodles in a bowl and cover with boiling water. Leave to stand for 20 minutes, stirring occasionally, or until tender. Drain and reserve. Meanwhile, blanch the broccoli in a saucepan of lightly salted boiling water for 2 minutes. Drain, refresh under cold running water and reserve.

2 Heat a large wok or frying pan, add the groundnut oil and heat until just smoking. Add the pork and stir-fry for 5 minutes, or until browned. Using a slotted spoon, remove the pork slices and reserve.

3 Mix together the soy sauce, lemon juice, sugar and chilli sauce, then reserve.

4 Add the ginger to the wok and stir-fry for 30 seconds. Add the garlic and chilli and stir-fry for 30 seconds.

5 Add the reserved broccoli and stir-fry for 3 minutes. Stir in the mangetout, pork and reserved noodles with the beaten eggs. Stir-fry for 5 minutes, or until heated through. Pour over the reserved sauce, toss well and turn into a warmed serving dish. Garnish and serve immediately.

1

2

5

Leek & Ham Risotto

INGREDIENTS

Serves 4

1 tbsp olive oil
25 g/1 oz margarine or butter
1 onion, peeled and finely chopped
3 leeks, trimmed and thinly sliced
1½ tbsp freshly chopped thyme
350 g/12 oz risotto rice
1.5 litres/2½ pints vegetable or
  chicken stock, heated
175 g/6 oz cooked ham
125 g/4 oz peas, thawed if frozen
25 g/1 oz Parmesan cheese, grated
salt and freshly ground black pepper

1 Heat the oil and half the margarine or butter together in a large saucepan. Add the onion and leeks and cook over a medium heat for 6–8 minutes, stirring occasionally, until soft and beginning to colour. Stir in the thyme and cook briefly.

2 Add the rice and stir well. Continue stirring over a medium heat for about 1 minute until the rice is glossy. Add a ladleful or two of the stock and stir well until the stock is absorbed. Continue adding stock, a ladleful at a time, and stirring well between additions, until about two thirds of the stock has been added.

3 Meanwhile, either chop or finely shred the ham, then add to the rice together with the peas. Continue adding ladlefuls of stock, as described in the previous step, until the rice is tender and the ham is heated through thoroughly. (Risotto should take about 20–25 minutes to cook, so taste it after this time – the rice should be creamy with just a slight bite to it. If it is not quite ready, continue adding the stock, a little at a time, and cook for a few more minutes. Stop as soon as it tastes ready, as you do not have to add all of the liquid.)

4 Add the remaining margarine or butter, sprinkle over the Parmesan cheese and season to taste with salt and pepper. When the cheese has softened, stir well to blend. Taste and adjust the seasoning, then serve immediately.

HELPFUL HINT

If you want to substitute, it is useful to know that 1 teaspoon dried herbs equals 1 tablespoon fresh herbs.

1

2

3

Meatballs with Olives

INGREDIENTS

Serves 4

1 large onion, peeled
2–3 garlic cloves, peeled
350 g/12 oz fresh, lean beef mince
2 tbsp fresh white or wholemeal
   breadcrumbs
3 tbsp freshly chopped basil
salt and freshly ground black pepper
2 tbsp olive oil
5 tbsp ready-made pesto
50 g/2 oz mascarpone cheese,
   chopped or grated
25 g/1 oz pitted black olives, halved
275 g/10 oz thick pasta noodles
freshly chopped flat-leaf parsley
fresh flat-leaf parsley sprigs,
   to garnish
freshly grated Parmesan cheese,
   to serve (optional)

1 Finely chop a quarter of the onion and place in a bowl with the garlic, beef mince, breadcrumbs, basil and seasoning to taste. With damp hands, bring the mixture together and shape into small balls about the size of an apricot.

2 Heat the olive oil in a frying pan and cook the meatballs for 8–10 minutes, turning occasionally, until browned and the beef is tender. Remove and drain on absorbent kitchen paper.

3 Slice the remaining onion, add to the pan and cook for 5 minutes until softened. Blend the pesto and mascarpone together, then stir into the pan with the olives. Bring to the boil, reduce the heat and return the meatballs to the pan. Simmer for 5–8 minutes until the sauce has thickened and the meatballs are cooked thoroughly.

4 Meanwhile, bring a large saucepan of lightly salted water to the boil and cook the noodles for 8–10 minutes until *al dente*. Drain the noodles, reserving 2 tablespoons of the cooking liquor. Return the noodles to the pan with the cooking liquor and pour in the sauce. Stir the noodles, then sprinkle with chopped parsley. Garnish with a few parsley sprigs and serve immediately with grated Parmesan cheese.

1

2

3

Steak & Kidney Stew

INGREDIENTS

Serves 4

1 tbsp olive oil
1 onion, peeled and chopped
2–3 garlic cloves, peeled and crushed
2 celery stalks, trimmed and sliced
450 g/1 lb stewing steak,
  trimmed and diced
2–4 lambs' kidneys, cored
  and chopped
2 tbsp plain flour
1 tbsp tomato purée
900 ml/1½ pints beef stock
salt and freshly ground black pepper
1 fresh bay leaf
2 large carrots, peeled and sliced
350 g/12 oz new potatoes, scrubbed
  and cut in half, or quarters if large
225 g/8 oz fresh spinach
  leaves, chopped

For the dumplings:

125 g/4 oz self-raising flour
50 g/2 oz shredded suet
1 tbsp freshly chopped mixed herbs

1 Heat the oil in a large, heavy-based saucepan, add the onion, garlic and celery and sauté for 5 minutes, or until browned. Remove from the pan with a slotted spoon and reserve.

2 Add the steak and kidneys to the pan and cook for 3–5 minutes until sealed, then return the onion mixture to the pan. Sprinkle in the flour and cook, stirring, for 2 minutes. Take off the heat, stir in the tomato purée, then the stock, and season to taste with salt and pepper. Add the bay leaf.

3 Return to the heat and bring to the boil, stirring occasionally. Add the carrots, then reduce the heat to a simmer and cover with a lid. Cook for 1½ hours, stirring occasionally. Reduce the heat if the liquid is evaporating quickly. Add the potatoes and cook for a further 30 minutes.

4 Place the flour, suet and herbs in a bowl and add a little seasoning. Add the 2–3 tablespoons water and mix to a stiff mixture. Using a little extra flour, shape into eight small balls. Place the dumplings on top of the stew, cover with the lid and continue to cook for 15 minutes, or until the meat is tender and the dumplings are well risen and fluffy. Stir in the spinach and leave to stand for 2 minutes, or until the spinach has wilted.

1

4

4

Moroccan Penne

INGREDIENTS

Serves 4

1 tbsp sunflower oil

1 red onion, peeled and chopped

2 garlic cloves, peeled and crushed

1 tbsp coriander seeds

$\frac{1}{4}$ tsp cumin seeds

$\frac{1}{4}$ tsp freshly grated nutmeg

450 g/1 lb fresh, lean lamb mince

1 aubergine, trimmed and diced

400 g can whole peeled
   tomatoes, chopped

300 ml/$\frac{1}{2}$ pint vegetable stock

125 g/4 oz ready-to-eat
   apricots, chopped

12 pitted black olives

salt and freshly ground black pepper

350 g/12 oz penne

1 tbsp toasted pine nuts,
   to garnish (optional)

1 Preheat the oven to 200°C/400°F/Gas Mark 6, 15 minutes before cooking. Heat the sunflower oil in a large, flameproof casserole dish. Add the onion and fry for 5 minutes, or until softened.

2 Using a pestle and mortar, pound the garlic, coriander seeds, cumin seeds and grated nutmeg together into a paste. Add to the onion and cook for 3 minutes.

3 Add the lamb mince to the casserole dish and fry, stirring with a wooden spoon, for 4–5 minutes until the mince has broken up and browned.

4 Add the aubergine to the mince and fry for 5 minutes. Stir in the chopped tomatoes and vegetable stock and bring to the boil. Add the apricots and olives, then season well with salt and pepper. Return to the boil, lower the heat and simmer for 15 minutes.

5 Add the penne to the casserole dish, stir well, then cover and place in the preheated oven. Cook for 10 minutes, then stir and return to the oven, uncovered, for a further 15–20 minutes until the pasta is *al dente*. Remove from the oven, sprinkle with toasted pine nuts, if using, and serve immediately.

2

4

5

Lamb Pilaf

INGREDIENTS

Serves 4

2 tbsp vegetable oil
25 g/1 oz flaked almonds
1 onion, peeled and finely chopped
1 carrot, peeled and finely chopped
1 celery stalk, trimmed and
   finely chopped
350 g/12 oz lamb, such as
   boneless shoulder or neck
   fillet, cut into chunks
1/4 tsp ground cinnamon
1/4 –1/2 tsp crushed chilli flakes
2 large tomatoes, skinned,
   deseeded and chopped
grated zest of 1 orange
300 g/11 oz easy-cook brown
   basmati rice
600 ml/1 pint vegetable or lamb stock
2 tbsp freshly snipped chives
3 tbsp freshly chopped coriander
salt and freshly ground
   black pepper

To garnish:

lemon slices
fresh coriander sprigs

1 Preheat the oven to 180°C/350°F/Gas Mark 4. Heat the oil in a flameproof casserole dish with a tight-fitting lid and add the almonds. Fry for about 1 minute until just starting to brown, stirring often. Add the onion, carrot and celery and cook gently for a further 8–10 minutes until soft and lightly browned.

2 Increase the heat and add the lamb. Cook for a further 5 minutes until the lamb has changed colour. Add the ground cinnamon and chilli flakes and stir briefly before adding the tomatoes and orange zest.

3 Stir and add the rice, then the stock. Bring slowly to the boil and cover tightly. Transfer to the preheated oven and cook for 30–35 minutes until the rice is tender and the stock is absorbed.

4 Remove from the oven and leave to stand for 5 minutes before stirring in the chives and coriander. Season to taste with salt and pepper. Garnish with the lemon slices and fresh coriander sprigs and serve immediately.

Mini Chicken Balls with Tagliatelle

INGREDIENTS

Serves 4

350 g/12 oz fresh chicken mince
25 g/1 oz sun-dried tomatoes, drained
  and finely chopped
salt and freshly ground black pepper
25 g/1 oz margarine or butter
1 tbsp vegetable oil
2 leeks, trimmed and
  diagonally sliced
125 g/4 oz frozen broad beans
300 ml/½ pint single cream
25 g/1 oz freshly grated Cheddar
  or Parmesan cheese
350 g/12 oz tagliatelle
4 medium eggs
fresh herbs, to garnish

1 Mix the chicken mince and tomatoes together and season to taste with salt and pepper. Divide the mixture into 32 pieces and roll into balls. Transfer to a baking sheet, cover and leave in the refrigerator for 1 hour.

2 Melt the margarine or butter in a large frying pan until sizzling, add the chicken balls and cook for 5 minutes, or until golden, turning occasionally (they need plenty of room for turning; if necessary, cook in two batches, halving the margarine or butter for each). Remove, drain on absorbent kitchen paper and keep warm.

3 Heat the oil in the pan, add the leeks and broad beans and cook, stirring, for 10 minutes, or until cooked and tender. Return the chicken balls to the pan, then stir in the cream and cheese and heat through.

4 Meanwhile, bring a large pan of lightly salted water to a rolling boil. Add the pasta and cook according to the packet instructions, or until *al dente*. Bring a separate frying pan full of water to the boil, crack in the eggs and simmer for 2–4 minutes until poached to personal preference.

5 Meanwhile, drain the pasta thoroughly and return to the pan. Pour the chicken balls and vegetable sauce over the pasta, toss lightly and heat through for 1–2 minutes. Arrange on warmed individual plates and top with the poached eggs. Garnish with fresh herbs and serve immediately.

Cheesy Chicken Burgers

INGREDIENTS

Serves 4

1 tbsp sunflower oil

1 small onion, peeled and finely chopped

1 garlic clove, peeled and crushed

½ red pepper, deseeded and
 finely chopped

350 g/12 oz fresh chicken mince

2 tbsp Greek yogurt

40 g/1½ oz fresh brown breadcrumbs

1 tbsp freshly chopped herbs,
 such as parsley or tarragon

50 g/2 oz Cheshire cheese, crumbled

salt and freshly ground black pepper

For the sweetcorn and carrot relish:

125 g/4 oz cooked sweetcorn
 kernels, drained

1 small carrot, peeled and grated

½ green chilli, deseeded and
 finely chopped

2 tsp white wine vinegar

2 tsp soft light brown sugar

To serve:

wholemeal or granary rolls

lettuce

sliced tomatoes

mixed salad leaves

1 Preheat the grill to medium. Heat the oil in a frying pan and gently cook the onion and garlic for 5 minutes. Add the red pepper and cook for 5 minutes. Transfer into a mixing bowl and add the chicken, yogurt, breadcrumbs, herbs and cheese and season to taste with salt and pepper. Mix well. Divide the mixture equally into six and shape into burgers. Cover and chill in the refrigerator for at least 20 minutes.

2 To make the relish, put all the ingredients in a small saucepan with 1 tablespoon water and heat gently, stirring occasionally, until all the sugar has dissolved. Cover and cook over a low heat for 2 minutes, then uncover and cook for a further minute, or until the relish is thick.

3 Place the burgers on a lightly oiled grill pan and cook under the preheated grill for 8–10 minutes on each side until browned and completely cooked through.

4 Warm the rolls, if liked, then split in half and fill with the burgers, lettuce, sliced tomatoes and the prepared relish. Serve with mixed salad leaves.

Potato & Goats' Cheese Tart

INGREDIENTS

Serves 6

275 g/10 oz prepared shortcrust
   pastry, thawed if frozen
plain flour, for dusting
550 g/1 lb 3 oz small, waxy potatoes
beaten egg, for brushing
2 tbsp tomato purée
¼ tsp chilli powder, or
   to taste
1 large egg
150 ml/¼ pint sour cream
150 ml/¼ pint milk
2 tbsp freshly snipped chives
salt and freshly ground black pepper
250 g/9 oz goats' cheese, sliced
salad and warm crusty bread,
   to serve

1 Preheat the oven to 190°C/375°F/Gas Mark 5, about 10 minutes before cooking. Roll the pastry out on a lightly floured surface and use to line a 23 cm/9 inch, fluted flan tin. Chill in the refrigerator for 30 minutes.

2 Scrub the potatoes, place in a large saucepan of lightly salted water and bring to the boil. Simmer for 10–15 minutes until the potatoes are tender. Drain and reserve until cool enough to handle.

3 Line the pastry case with greaseproof paper and baking beans or crumpled foil and bake blind in the preheated oven for 15 minutes. Remove from the oven and discard the paper and beans or foil. Brush the base with a little beaten egg, then return to the oven and cook for a further 5 minutes. Remove from the oven.

4 Cut the potatoes into 1 cm/½ inch thick slices; reserve. Spread the tomato purée over the base of the pastry case, sprinkle with the chilli powder, then arrange the potato slices on top in a decorative pattern.

5 Beat together the egg, sour cream, milk and chives, then season to taste with salt and pepper. Pour over the potatoes. Arrange the goats' cheese on top of the potatoes. Bake in the preheated oven for 30 minutes until golden brown and set. Serve immediately with salad and warm bread.

HELPFUL HINT

Goats' cheese can tend to be a little acidic, so it is best to try to choose a creamy variety, which will mellow even more once baked.

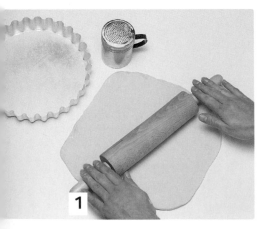

1

3

4

Mixed Grain Pilaf

INGREDIENTS

Serves 4

2 tbsp olive oil
1 garlic clove, peeled and crushed
½ tsp ground turmeric
125 g/4 oz mixed long-grain
   and wild rice
50 g/2 oz red lentils
300 ml/½ pint vegetable stock
200 g can chopped tomatoes
5 cm/2 inch cinnamon stick
salt and freshly ground black pepper
400 g can mixed beans, drained
   and rinsed

For the omelette:

15 g/½ oz margarine or butter
1 bunch spring onions, trimmed
   and finely sliced
3 medium eggs
4 tbsp freshly chopped herbs,
   such as parsley and chervil
fresh dill sprigs, to garnish

1 Heat 1 tablespoon of the oil in a saucepan. Add the garlic and turmeric and cook for a few seconds. Stir in the rice and lentils. Add the stock, tomatoes and cinnamon. Season to taste with salt and pepper. Stir once and bring to the boil. Lower the heat, cover and simmer for 20 minutes until most of the stock is absorbed and the rice and lentils are tender. Stir in the beans, replace the lid and leave to stand for 2–3 minutes to allow the beans to heat through.

2 While the rice is cooking, heat the remaining oil and the margarine or butter in a frying pan. Add the spring onions and cook for 4–5 minutes until soft. Lightly beat the eggs with 2 tablespoons of the herbs, then season with salt and pepper.

3 Pour the egg mixture over the spring onions. Stir gently with a spatula over a low heat, drawing the mixture from the sides to the centre as the omelette sets. When almost set, stop stirring and cook for about 30 seconds until golden underneath.

4 Remove the omelette from the pan, roll up and slice into thin strips. Fluff the rice up with a fork and remove the cinnamon stick. Spoon onto serving plates, top with strips of omelette and the remaining chopped herbs. Garnish with sprigs of dill and serve.

Layered Cheese & Herb Potato Cake

INGREDIENTS

Serves 4

450 g/1 lb waxy potatoes
2 tbsp freshly snipped chives
1 tbsp freshly chopped parsley
125 g/4 oz mature Cheddar cheese
1 medium egg, beaten
1 tsp paprika
75 g/3 oz fresh white breadcrumbs
50 g/2 oz almonds, toasted and
  roughly chopped
salt and freshly ground black pepper
40 g/1½ oz margarine or
  butter, melted
mixed salad or steamed
  vegetables, to serve

1 Preheat the oven to 180°C/350°F/Gas Mark 4. Lightly oil and line the base of an 18 cm/7 inch round cake tin with greaseproof paper or baking parchment.

2 Peel and thinly slice the potatoes and reserve. Stir the chives, parsley, cheese and egg together in a small bowl and reserve. Mix the paprika into the breadcrumbs.

3 Sprinkle the almonds over the base of the lined tin. Cover with half the potatoes, arranging them in layers, then sprinkle with the paprika breadcrumb mixture and season to taste with salt and pepper. Spoon the cheese and herb mixture over the breadcrumbs with a little more seasoning, then arrange the remaining potatoes on top. Drizzle over the melted margarine or butter and press the surface down firmly.

4 Bake in the preheated oven for 1¼ hours, or until golden and cooked through – check that the potatoes are tender all the way through by pushing a thin skewer through the centre. If the potatoes are still a little hard and the top is already brown enough, loosely cover with foil and continue cooking until done.

5 Let the tin stand for 10 minutes before carefully turning out and serving in thick wedges. Serve immediately with salad or freshly cooked vegetables.

2

3

3

Vegetarian Cassoulet

INGREDIENTS

Serves 4

225 g/8 oz dried haricot beans,
 soaked overnight
2 medium onions
1 bay leaf
1.5 litres/2½ pints cold water
550 g/1 lb 3 oz large potatoes, peeled
 and cut into 1 cm/½ inch slices
5 tsp olive oil
1 large garlic clove, peeled
 and crushed
2 leeks, trimmed and sliced
200 g/7 oz canned whole peeled
 tomatoes, chopped
1 tsp dark muscovado sugar
1 tbsp freshly chopped thyme
2 tbsp freshly chopped parsley
salt and freshly ground
 black pepper
3 courgettes, trimmed and sliced

For the topping:

50 g/2 oz fresh white breadcrumbs
25 g/1 oz Cheddar cheese,
 finely grated

1 Preheat the oven to 180°C/350°F/Gas Mark 4, 10 minutes before required. Drain the beans and rinse under cold running water, then place in a saucepan. Peel one of the onions and add to the beans with the bay leaf. Pour in the water. Bring to a rapid boil and cook for 10 minutes, then turn down the heat, cover and simmer for 50 minutes, or until the beans are almost tender. Drain the beans, reserving the liquor, but discarding the onion and bay leaf.

2 Cook the potatoes in a pan of lightly salted boiling water for 6–7 minutes until almost tender when tested with the point of a knife. Drain and reserve.

3 Peel and chop the remaining onion. Heat the oil in a frying pan and cook the onion, garlic and leeks for 10 minutes until softened. Stir in the tomatoes, sugar, thyme and parsley. Stir in the beans with 300 ml/½ pint of the reserved liquor and season to taste. Simmer, uncovered, for 5 minutes.

4 Layer the potato slices, courgettes and ladlefuls of the bean mixture in a large casserole dish. To make the topping, mix together the breadcrumbs and cheese and sprinkle over the top. Bake in the preheated oven for 40 minutes, or until the vegetables are cooked through and the topping is golden. Serve.

1

3

4

Sicilian Baked Aubergine

INGREDIENTS

Serves 4

2 aubergines, trimmed

2 tbsp olive oil

4 large, ripe tomatoes

2 celery stalks, trimmed

2 shallots, peeled and finely chopped

1½ tsp tomato purée

25 g/1 oz pitted green olives

25 g/1 oz pitted black olives

salt and freshly ground black pepper

1 tbsp white wine vinegar

2 tsp caster sugar

1 tbsp freshly chopped basil,
  to garnish

mixed salad leaves, to serve

1 Preheat the oven to 200°C/400°F/Gas Mark 6, 15 minutes before baking. Cut the aubergines into small cubes and place on an oiled baking tray. Sprinkle with 1½ tablespoons of the oil.

2 Cover the tray with foil and bake in the preheated oven for 15–20 minutes until soft. Reserve to allow the aubergine to cool.

3 Using a sharp knife, score crosses in the tops of the tomatoes. Place the tomatoes and the celery in a large bowl and cover with boiling water. Remove the tomatoes from the bowl when their skins begin to peel away. Remove the skins, then deseed and chop the flesh into small pieces. Remove the celery from the bowl of water, chop finely and reserve.

4 Pour the remaining oil into a nonstick saucepan, add the chopped shallots and fry gently for 2–3 minutes until soft. Add the celery, tomatoes, tomato purée and olives. Season to taste with salt and pepper. Simmer gently for 3–4 minutes.

5 Add the vinegar, sugar and cooled aubergine to the pan and heat gently for 2–3 minutes until all the ingredients are well blended. Reserve to allow the aubergine mixture to cool. When cool, garnish with the chopped basil and serve cold with salad leaves.

HELPFUL HINT

Alternatively, to peel tomatoes easily, hold the tomatoes over a gas flame with a fork for a few seconds, turning until the skin is slightly blackened and blistered. Cool, then peel.

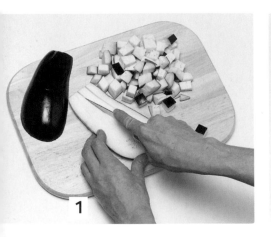

Carrot & Parsnip Terrine

INGREDIENTS

Serves 8–10

550 g/1 lb 3 oz carrots, peeled
  and chopped

450 g/1 lb parsnips, peeled
  and chopped

6 tbsp crème fraîche

450 g/1 lb spinach, rinsed

1 tbsp brown sugar

1 tbsp freshly chopped parsley

½ tsp freshly grated nutmeg

salt and freshly ground black pepper

6 medium eggs

fresh basil sprigs, to garnish

For the tomato coulis:

450 g/1 lb ripe tomatoes,
  deseeded and chopped

1 medium onion, peeled
  and finely chopped

1 Preheat the oven to 200°C/400°F/Gas Mark 6, 15 minutes before baking. Oil and line a 900 g/2 lb loaf tin with nonstick baking paper. Cook the carrots and parsnips in boiling salted water for 10–15 minutes until very tender. Drain and purée separately. Add 2 tablespoons of the crème fraîche to both the carrots and the parsnips.

2 Steam the spinach for 5–10 minutes until very tender. Drain and squeeze out as much liquid as possible, then stir in the remaining crème fraîche.

3 Add the brown sugar to the carrot purée, the parsley to the parsnip mixture and the nutmeg to the spinach. Season all to taste with salt and pepper.

4 Beat 2 of the eggs, add to the spinach and turn into the tin. Add another 2 beaten eggs to the carrot mixture and layer carefully on top of the spinach. Beat the remaining eggs into the parsnip purée and layer on top of the terrine. Place the tin in a baking dish and pour in enough hot water to come halfway up the sides of the tin. Bake for 1 hour until a skewer inserted into the centre comes out clean. Leave to cool for at least 30 minutes. Run a sharp knife around the edges. Turn out onto a dish, garnish with basil sprigs and reserve.

5 Make the coulis by simmering the tomatoes and onion together for 5–10 minutes until slightly thickened. Season to taste. Blend well in a liquidiser and serve with the terrine.

3

4

5

Roasted Butternut Squash

INGREDIENTS

Serves 4

2 small butternut squash
4 garlic cloves, peeled and crushed
2 tbsp olive oil
salt and freshly ground
 black pepper
4 medium-size leeks, trimmed,
 cleaned and thinly sliced
300 g can cannellini beans,
 drained and rinsed
125 g/4 oz fine French beans, halved
1 tbsp wholegrain mustard, or to taste
150 ml/¼ pint vegetable stock
50 g/2 oz rocket or watercress
2 tbsp freshly snipped chives
fresh chives, to garnish

To serve:

4 tbsp fromage frais
mixed salad

1 Preheat the oven to 200°C/400°F/Gas Mark 6, 15 minutes before roasting. Cut the butternut squash in half lengthways and scoop out all of the seeds.

2 Score the squash in a diamond pattern with a sharp knife. Mix the garlic with 1 tablespoon of the olive oil and brush over the cut surfaces of the squash. Season well with salt and pepper. Put on a baking sheet and roast for 40 minutes until tender.

3 Heat the remaining oil in a saucepan and fry the leeks for 5 minutes.

4 Add the drained cannellini beans, French beans, wholegrain mustard and vegetable stock. Bring to the boil and simmer gently for 5 minutes until the French beans are tender.

5 Remove from the heat and stir in the rocket or watercress and chives. Season well. Remove the squash from the oven and allow to cool for 5 minutes. Spoon in the bean mixture. Garnish with a few snipped chives and serve immediately with the fromage frais and a mixed salad.

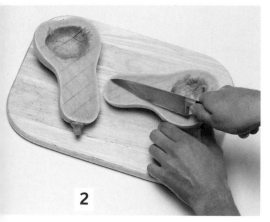

2

4

5

Bacon & Tomato Breakfast Twist

INGREDIENTS

Serves 4

450 g/1 lb strong white flour
½ tsp salt
7 g sachet easy-blend dried yeast
300 ml/½ pint warm milk
15 g/½ oz margarine or butter, melted

For the filling:

225 g/8 oz back bacon, rind removed
15 g/½ oz margarine or butter, melted
175 g/6 oz ripe tomatoes, peeled,
  deseeded, chopped
freshly ground black pepper

To finish:

beaten egg, to glaze
2 tsp medium oatmeal

1 Preheat the oven to 200°C/400°F/Gas Mark 6, 15 minutes before baking. Sift the flour and salt into a large bowl. Stir in the yeast and make a well in the centre. Pour in the milk and margarine or butter and mix to a soft dough.

2 Knead on a lightly floured surface for 10 minutes until smooth and elastic. Put in an oiled bowl, cover with clingfilm and leave to rise in a warm place for 1 hour until doubled in size.

3 Cook the bacon under a hot grill for 5–6 minutes, turning once, until crisp. Leave to cool, then roughly chop.

4 Knead the dough again for a minute or two. Roll it out to a 25 x 33 cm/10 x 13 inch rectangle. Cut in half lengthways. Lightly brush with margarine or butter, then scatter with the bacon, tomatoes and black pepper, leaving a 1 cm/½ inch margin around the edges. Brush the edges of the dough with beaten egg, then roll up each rectangle lengthways.

5 Place the two rolls side by side and twist together, pinching the ends to seal. Transfer to an oiled baking sheet and loosely cover with oiled clingfilm. Leave to rise in a warm place for 30 minutes. Brush with the beaten egg and sprinkle with the oatmeal. Bake in the preheated oven for about 30 minutes until golden brown and hollow-sounding when tapped on the base. Serve the bread warm in thick slices.

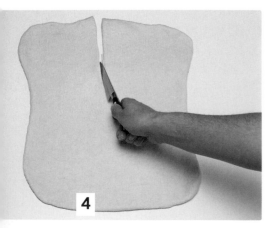

4

4

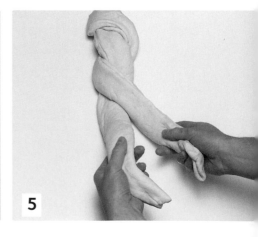

5

Lemon Surprise

INGREDIENTS

Serves 4

75 g/3 oz margarine or butter
175 g/6 oz caster sugar
3 medium eggs, separated
75 g/3 oz self-raising flour
450 ml/³/₄ pint milk
juice of 2 lemons
juice of 1 orange
2 tsp icing sugar
lemon twists, to decorate (optional)
sliced strawberries, to serve (optional)

1 Preheat the oven to 190°C/375°F/Gas Mark 5. Lightly oil a deep, ovenproof dish.

2 Beat together the margarine or butter and sugar until pale and fluffy. Add the egg yolks, one at a time, with 1 tablespoon of the flour. Beat well after each addition. Once added, stir in the remaining flour. Stir in the milk, 4 tablespoons of the lemon juice and 3 tablespoons of the orange juice.

3 Whisk the egg whites until stiff and fold into the pudding mixture with a metal spoon or rubber spatula until well combined. Pour into the prepared dish.

4 Stand the dish in a roasting tin and pour in just enough boiling water to come halfway up the sides of the dish. Bake in the preheated oven for 45 minutes until well risen and spongy to the touch.

5 Remove the pudding from the oven and sprinkle with the icing sugar. If liked, decorate with the lemon twists and serve immediately with the strawberries.

2

3

4

Carrot Cake

INGREDIENTS

Cuts into 8 slices

200 g/7 oz plain flour

½ tsp ground cinnamon

½ tsp freshly grated nutmeg

1 tsp baking powder

1 tsp bicarbonate of soda

150 g/5 oz dark
   muscovado sugar

200 ml/7 fl oz vegetable oil

3 medium eggs

225 g/8 oz carrots, peeled
   and roughly grated

50 g/2 oz chopped walnuts

For the icing:

175 g/6 oz cream cheese

finely grated zest of 1 orange

1 tbsp orange juice

1 tsp vanilla extract

125 g/4 oz icing sugar

1 Preheat the oven to 150°C/300°F/Gas Mark 2, 10 minutes before baking. Lightly oil and line the base of a 15 cm/6 inch, deep, square cake tin with greaseproof paper or baking parchment.

2 Sift the flour, spices, baking powder and bicarbonate of soda together into a large bowl. Stir in the dark muscovado sugar and mix together.

3 Lightly whisk the oil and eggs together, then gradually stir into the flour and sugar mixture. Stir well. Add the carrots and walnuts. Mix thoroughly, then pour into the prepared cake tin. Bake in the preheated oven for 1¼ hours, or until light and springy to the touch and a skewer inserted into the centre of the cake comes out clean.

4 Remove from the oven and allow to cool in the tin for 5 minutes, then turn out onto a wire rack. Leave until cold.

5 To make the icing, beat together the cream cheese, orange zest, orange juice and vanilla extract. Sift the icing sugar and stir into the cream cheese mixture.

6 When the cake is cold, discard the lining paper, spread the cream cheese icing over the top of the cake and serve cut into squares.

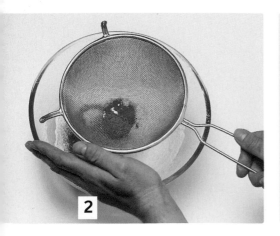

2

3

5

Gingerbread

INGREDIENTS

Cuts into 8 slices

175 g/6 oz margarine or butter
225 g/8 oz black treacle
50 g/2 oz dark muscovado sugar
350 g/12 oz plain flour
2 tsp ground ginger
150 ml/¼ pint milk, warmed
2 medium eggs
1 tsp bicarbonate of soda
1 piece stem ginger in syrup
1 tbsp stem ginger syrup

1 Preheat the oven to 150°C/300°F/Gas Mark 2, 10 minutes before baking. Lightly oil and line the base of a 20.5 cm/8 inch, deep, round cake tin with greaseproof paper or baking parchment.

2 In a saucepan, gently heat the margarine or butter, black treacle and sugar together, stirring occasionally, until the butter melts. Leave to cool slightly.

3 Sift the flour and ground ginger into a large bowl. Make a well in the centre, then pour in the treacle mixture. Reserve 1 tablespoon of the milk, then pour the rest into the treacle mixture. Stir together lightly until mixed.

4 Beat the eggs together, then stir into the mixture.

5 Dissolve the bicarbonate of soda in the remaining 1 tablespoon of warmed milk and add to the mixture. Beat until well mixed and free of lumps. Pour into the prepared tin and bake in the preheated oven for 1 hour, or until well risen and a skewer inserted into the centre comes out clean.

6 Cool in the tin, then remove. Slice the stem ginger into thin slivers and sprinkle over the cake. Drizzle with the syrup and serve.

2

5

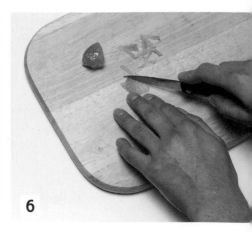

6

Step-by-Step, Practical Recipes Cooking on a Budget: Tips & Hints

Helpful Hint

Be aware that your budget is not always going to be as simple as, say, £5 per meal – that may not account for snacks or desserts. Instead, before you set out to go food shopping, set a budget that you will not exceed. Your assigned budget must be realistic; many people often set unrealistically small targets, which can cause further problems. If you know you have a celebration coming up, make sure you factor it into your budget; you could save a little each week in advance so that the extra expense of the occasion does not break the bank.

Helpful Hint

Cut down on the amount of food, and therefore money, you waste by cutting back on any foods which seem to be consistently left in the refrigerator until they have passed their use-by date. Also think about how many meals you will be eating at home for the week for which you do your shop and set some rough meal plans of what you will cook; if you will be eating more at lunchtimes than evening meals it is not a good idea to buy lots of ingredients for big evening meals.

Helpful Hint

By assessing your finances at the beginning of each month you can make sure you cover all important costs whilst remaining aware of how much money you will have left to spend on food. This may help you to decide how often you can afford to eat out and whether you may need to cut back on treats for a while until you are on top of your finances again.

Helpful Hint

Making a list before you do your supermarket shop is very important – it not only helps you remember those essential items that you really need to stock up on, but will also stop you from impulse buying excessive amounts of food that you don't really need and are not part of your weekly meal plan. If you have any money-off coupons or loyalty cards make sure that you take these along too.

Tasty Tip

Cooking dishes based around versatile staples such as pasta, rice and potatoes is a great way to save money whilst still producing tasty and filling meals. To make meals go further you can also use pulses such as beans, peas and lentils to thicken up without having to add more meat, which can get expensive; if using this tactic, choose dried rather than canned pulses as they tend to be cheaper.

Helpful Hint

Make the most of special offers when you see them in the supermarket, but only if you will actually end up using the food rather than wasting it. Think about whether the items will keep for a long time, such as canned goods, or are suitable for home freezing. If it is fresh vegetables that are on offer you could cook them into a vegetable curry or pasta sauce which can then be frozen and eaten another time.

Tasty Tip

If you are cooking a fish dish, look out for smoked haddock or mackerel. Both of these are relatively cheap fish varieties which are still excellent sources of minerals, oils and vitamins. Dishes such as Smoked Haddock Tart (*see* page 2) and Smoked Haddock Kedgeree (*see* page 6) make good use of affordable and filling staples, such as pastry and rice, to create a delicious way of incorporating the essential nutrients of fish into your diet.

Tasty Tip

Certain dishes, such as Pork Fried Noodles (*see* page 10), are excellent when it comes to using up leftover meat, perhaps from the Sunday Roast. If you are using cooked meat, reduce the cooking time accordingly, but make sure that it is piping hot before serving.

Tasty Tip

Dried herbs often go further and last longer than fresh herbs. They can be easily added to most recipes to give some added flavour and draw out the taste of other foods. These are a good item to ensure you have in the cupboard at all times as they can liven up meals and compensate for any taste that may be lost from spending less on other ingredients.

First published in 2013 by
FLAME TREE PUBLISHING LTD
Crabtree Hall, Crabtree Lane, Fulham,
London, SW6 6TY, United Kingdom
www.flametreepublishing.com

NOTE: Recipes using uncooked eggs should be avoided by infants, the elderly, pregnant women and anyone suffering from an illness.

18 17 16 15 14 13   10 9 8 7 6 5 4 3 2 1

ISBN: 978-0-85775-856-9

ACKNOWLEDGEMENTS: Authors: Catherine Atkinson, Juliet Barker, Gina Steer, Vicki Smallwood, Carol Tennant, Mari Mererid Williams, Elizabeth Wolf-Cohen and Simone Wright. Photography: Colin Bowling, Paul Forrester and Stephen Brayne. Home Economists and Stylists: Jacqueline Bellefontaine, Mandy Phipps, Vicki Smallwood and Penny Stephens. Some props supplied by Barbara Stewart at Surfaces. Publisher and Creative Director: Nick Wells. Editorial: Catherine Taylor, Laura Bulbeck, Esme Chapman, Emma Chafer, Gina Steer and Karen Fitzpatrick. Design and Production: Chris Herbert, Mike Spender and Helen Wall.